DIVERSI

T0152333

Diversity Rules

PETER W. WOOD

BOOKS

NEW YORK · LONDON

First American edition published in 2019 by Encounter Books,
an activity of Encounter for Culture and Education, Inc.,
a nonprofit, tax-exempt corporation.
Encounter Books website address: www.encounterbooks.com

Manufactured in the United States and printed on
acid-free paper. The paper used in this publication meets
the minimum requirements of ANSI/NISO Z39.48–1992
(R 1997) (*Permanence of Paper*).

FIRST AMERICAN EDITION

LIBRARY OF CONGRESS
CATALOGING-IN-PUBLICATION DATA
IS AVAILABLE

I F I WERE TO WRITE another long book on *diversity*, I would take as my model Alexis de Tocqueville's *Democracy in America* and title it *Diversity in America*. And I would set out to capture the transformation of a republic founded on the ideals of freedom and equality into a regime scared into submission by the fear of being called a "racist." This all-purpose term of opprobrium is *diversity's* way of silencing dissent and forcing its way ahead wherever its leaders choose to take it.

But this isn't that book. Instead, it is my commentary on what has happened since 2003, when I authored *Diversity: The Invention of a Concept*.

Diversity is the grown child still living at home. He is old enough by now to move out, but he just hasn't gotten around to it. Moreover, the United States Supreme Court ruled in 2003 that he could stay another twenty-five years. Let's see: that would be June 2028, when he'll be exactly fifty years old. I suspect at that point he will want to stay put.

He will be fifty because the *diversity* doctrine as we have come to know it was born at the Supreme Court in June 1978. That's when the Court handed down its decision in the case of *Bakke vs. The University of California*, and Justice Lewis Powell freelanced an opinion that put *diversity* on the map. Powell said that the Medical School at the University of California Davis had no business offering racial preferences to some applicants in an effort to right historical injustices. But if the University had justified its racial preferences as a way to achieve the educational benefits of *diversity*, Powell, for one, might have reached a different conclusion.

No other Justice agreed with Powell on this point, and his opinion could easily have rolled off the table like a loose marble to be swept away when the cleaners arrived. But as it happened, colleges and universities were looking for a new way to justify the use of race in college admissions. They feared the Supreme Court would go beyond *Bakke* and rule all racial preferences unconstitutional.

That put the concept of "diversity" into play in American higher education. By the early 1980s, campus offices of "affirmative action" were rapidly being renamed *diversity* offices. Moreover, Powell's awkwardly written opinion gave way to a more expansive version of the idea. The opinion, after all, stereotyped members of minority groups as walking billboards for the views he imagined were characteristic of those groups. Black students were supposed to show up enunciating "black viewpoints" for the edification of non-black students. Powell explicitly justified favoritism toward black students as a way to enhance the educational experience of white students. He rejected entirely the idea that such favoritism could be founded on anything else, such as compensating minority students for historic grievances or overcoming a history of racial discrimination.

Powell's reasoning and his rhetoric were of limited use to the evangelists of *diversity*, but they swooned over the basic concept: a simple, memorable word that could stand for all sorts of things besides racial preferences in admissions. *Diversity*, for example, could also mean respect for the world's many cultures and revamping the curriculum in that light; hiring faculty members who "look like" the students; and even segregating students into racial groups – the better to serve their supposed group needs.

By the mid-eighties, *diversity* was the hottest idea in American education, and it was poised for breakout into the culture at large. In 1987, a misread report from the Hudson Institute stampeded corporate America towards the *diversity* cliff. The report seemed to say that by the turn of the century, standard-issue white workers would be a rapidly dwindling minority. The future belonged to those companies that got with the *diversity* program immediately. Overnight a new profession of "diversity consultants" was born.

If you have read *Diversity: The Invention of a Concept*, you have already enjoyed the scenic tour of what happened during those years. The book left off on the eve of the Supreme Court's decision in another race-preferences-in-college-admissions case, *Grutter v. Bollinger*. I dared hope at the end of the book that the Court would ring down the curtain on twenty-five years of Powell-inspired *diversity* folly. Justice Sandra Day O'Connor, however, disappointed me. She not only promised another twenty-five years of *diversity* folly, but she also gave the concept something that Powell had been unable to do: the kiss of legitimacy of a majority Supreme Court decision.

Liberty, Equality, Diversity

O'Connor's opinion has been ably dissected by many others, including four of her own colleagues on the Court. As with Powell's opinion in *Bakke*, however, the significance of O'Connor's validation of the *diversity* end-run on the Equal Protection clause of the Fourteenth Amendment far exceeds its particular legal applications. *Grutter* permits colleges and universities to apply racial preferences in student admissions provided they dress the preferences in suitable camouflage as the pursuit of *diversity*. But *Grutter* also gave ferocious new power to what we now call identity politics.

Diversity before *Grutter* was a creed ardently promoted by campus activists and increasingly taken to heart by college administrators. It was also a catchy idea that had been taken up without any serious reflection in many domains of American culture. Business, entertainment, sports, churches, and consumers were all attracted to aspects of the diversity doctrine. But *diversity* was still something new and a little unfamiliar.

Americans understand that our nation was founded on the principles of liberty and equality. Americans also understand that liberty and equality sometimes conflict. Perfect liberty seldom produces perfect equality. Some use their liberty to get rich. Some use their insistence on equality in a manner that cuts against others' liberties. Americans have long struggled to find the best ways to accommodate both ideals. *Diversity*, however, is something different: a third thing that in crucial ways undermines both liberty and equality.

Diversity undermines liberty because it takes away our basic freedom to decide for ourselves who we are. To be assigned to a racial or ethnic group that represents and supposedly speaks for me is to obstruct my right to free expression and my ability to craft my own identity. Or if self-definition doesn't match your sense of liberty, think of *diversity* as something that restricts our choices and opportunities by imposing a grid of unchosen racial, ethnic, or sexual group alliances. *Diversity* demands that individuals inwardly believe in and outwardly support specific views about race and gender in order to win acceptance in society.

Diversity also undermines equality, because it strips from the individual equality before the law and substitutes the pseudo-equality of group rights. These aren't small erosions of traditional rights, but major efforts to bulldoze those rights. Every time an American is asked to check a box on a form declaring himself white, black, Hispanic, Native American, or something else, he is permitting someone else to make decisions based on his race. He is sacrificing a bit of his autonomy. When a student applies for admission to college as an African-American or a construction company applies for a government contract as minority-owned, the student or the company is locked into the world of group identity. Calculations of self-interest henceforth have to be filtered through group interest.

To be sure, group interests were not invented in 1978, or in 2003. Our Founders, and many generations since, were well aware of the advantages that could accrue to people based on ethnic or tribal allegiance, and the disadvantages to the nation as a whole if such allegiances could run unchecked. Ethnic politics have always been with us. The *diversity* doctrine, however, turns what almost everyone agreed was a weakness of American democracy into a supposed strength. We are asked – endlessly – to "celebrate" *diversity*. And the *diversity* we are asked to celebrate isn't the mere abundance of social and cultural differences subsumed into the national fabric, but the differences that cannot and should not be subsumed: the group identities that remain primary loyalties.

Group interests weren't invented yesterday, but many of the groups claiming group interest are novelties, created by combining and repackaging various discontents. How did the great variety of Latin American cultures crystalize as "Latinx" people? Where in history did the congeries of sexual nonconformists ever before convene as LGBTQ? The invented quality of many of the grievance groups isn't incidental to *diversity*. The logic of the doctrine demands that it find new frontiers: new groups that parcel themselves into ever-more implausible categories to turn status into power. If a brand new category is hard to invent, *diversity* advocates can combine existing ones. This goes under the heading "intersectionality." If being black doesn't produce sufficient *diversity* points, try black and female, or black, female, and handicapped. Intersectionality multiplies the opportunities for grievance.

Diversity is all about factionalism, and about turning factionalism from a necessary evil to a positive good. *Diversity* advocates, or "diversiphiles" (I called them this in 2003 and the word has had a modest success in the years since), are often eager to assert they support a larger unity made up of disparate parts. When speaking in this mode, diversiphiles have two favorite metaphors. *Diversity* is like a quilt, pieced together of many parts that do not lose their distinctiveness when stitched together. Or *diversity* is like a salad bowl, in which the ingredients are tossed together to create a healthy whole.

These invocations of the unity that *diversity* can inspire have their tactical purposes and their psychological appeals. Tactically, they help to fend off the criticism that diversity is a justification for a racial spoils system. Psychologically, they offer the winsome prospect of good feeling among identity groups that might seem not all that friendly to one another. *Diversity* sells better as a benign invitation to an all-for-one-and-one-for-all picnic in the park, where we sit on the *diver-*

sity quilt and eat our vegetables together. Above all, *diversity* is not a "melting pot." The effort to assimilate outsiders to mainstream American culture is, in the eyes of diversiphiles, an offense against their cultural distinctiveness.

The quilt/salad bowl kindergarten version of *diversity*, alas, is pretty far from the real thing. Mostly what diversiphiles do is assert their grievances. Each group in the ever-expanding *diversity* alliance has its own history of injustices visited on past and sometimes current members. The legacy of these injustices transcends time and space. The hurt inflicted on people sold into slavery by West African kingdoms in the seventeenth century wears on the souls of distant descendants in the twenty-first century. The oppression experienced by women under millennia of "patriarchy" resurfaces in the lives of successful women today. The fully public and accepted gay individual of today is invited to claim ownership of the suffering of his closeted counterparts of the 1950s. Every "diverse" group has its story, its fallen heroes, and its landmarks. And from this soil grows resentment and demands for restitution.

Of course, some individuals who could play the diversity game decline the invitation. They choose not to be professional victims.

Diversity can, when convenient, pretend to be nice, but at its core it is a grudge match. It stands in deep opposition to American culture, which it treats as compromised and corrupt. The "winners" don't deserve their "privilege." They gained their advantages by means of malice and exploitation. *Diversity* is the summons to the exploited to set matters right. And it is a counsel to the heirs of the exploiters that they have one last chance to make amends.

My Type

The reader will have noticed by now my persistent italicization of the word *diversity*. This is a carryover from my book, in which I insisted that the modern *diversity* doctrine should be rigorously distinguished from the other meanings of the word. America was diverse long before it became *diverse*. The Roman-typeface word diversity refers to the real diversity of people that Americans encountered from the very beginning of European contact with the New World and that has persisted in the five-plus centuries since. That diversity sometimes brought conflict, sometimes mutual avoidance, and sometimes a rich intermingling. But diversity in this plain sense was not a positive or a negative. It was merely a fact. What was to be done about the fact depended on circumstances. There was no comprehensive edict that diversity was inherently good and must be respected, preserved, or turned into a rationale for a particular redistribution of social goods, such as access to college.

Diversity – back to italics – by contrast, has lost its plain descriptive sense of mere variety and become instead code for a social order organized as a hierarchy of victimization. The more victimized a group can claim to be, the higher its status in the *diversity* world. This hierarchy, of course, sets victim groups against each other in the struggle for relative status. Where exactly do LGBTQ people stand relative to Hispanics or Muslim Americans? There is no official scorekeeper, but it is not hard to see the competition. Right now advocates for the transgendered are in conflict with certain leaders of the feminist movement. So much for the quilt and the salad bowl.

Diversity is also part of a family of related words, among them *multiculturalism, inclusion, social justice,* and *equity.* These represent shades of meaning that are sometimes useful to distinguish, and I generally rely on context in this short essay rather than bog things down with formal definitions. *Diversity* and multiculturalism have an especially close affinity. *Diversity* points to a rationale for favoring particular groups; *multiculturalism* conjures a vision of modern states that have accommodated themselves to a condition in which cultural divisiveness is the norm. *Inclusion* is a sly word that generally means lowering standards to accommodate those who can't meet them. *Social justice* is the doctrine of elevating group identity as the principal ground for redistributing wealth and other social goods. *Equity* is the idea that those who have less of a particular good have a moral claim on others for a larger share.

Diversity Today

At the end of July 2019, the Democratic Congressional Campaign Committee (DCCC) received the resignations of six of its top staff members, including its executive director Allison Jaslow. The issue was that they were insufficiently "diverse." A week before, the Congressional Black Caucus and the Congressional Hispanic Caucus had denounced Cheri Bustos, the chairwoman of the DCCC, for "short-changing minorities by excluding them from her senior staff."[1]

"There is not one person of color – black or brown, that I'm aware of – at any position of authority or decision-making in the DCCC," said Rep. Marcia Fudge (D-Ohio), a former chairwoman of the Congressional Black Caucus.

"It is shocking, it is shocking, and something needs to be done about it."[2]

Bustos promptly threw her senior staff under the *diversity* bus. In the political calculations of the Democratic Party, appeasing the demands of blacks and Hispanics for patronage positions is a priority.

The surprise, if any, in this shakeup is how undressed the racial and ethnic politics were. Two identity-labeled groups demanded a large share of the spoils of office and the Party leadership met those demands almost faster than the time it takes to get from Union Station to Capitol Hill.

Plainly, *diversity* can open sticky doors.

Bustos is certainly no stranger to identity politics. She is a four-term Representative from Illinois' Seventeenth Congressional District and has made a big deal of being the first woman elected to that position. She has argued that Congress needs to have more women, to draw attention to the issue of sexual assault. She also served briefly on a committee in Illinois, "to lead a statewide discussion about the role of women in the Democratic party and how to 'change the culture of politics.'"[3] She resigned from that position after the House Ethics Committee counseled her to. Three of the six staffers whom she purged from the DCCC were women.

Some kinds of *diversity* count more than others.

A month earlier, in June 2019, the California Department of Education issued the *Ethnic Studies Model Curriculum Guidelines* for 2020. An official comment period from June to August 15 brought a national deluge of ridicule down of the Model Guidelines – a measure, perhaps, of the large division between new diversiphile orthodoxy and public opinion. Williamson Evers, a research fellow at the Hoover Institute, took to *The Wall Street Journal* to warn, "California Wants to Teach Yours Kids That Capitalism Is Bad."[4] The *Los Angeles Times* reported that "the draft sparked opposition among many Jewish groups, who have been joined by organizations representing Armenians, Greeks, Hindus and Koreans in calling for changes."[5] The State Board of Education, which was initially enthusiastic about the guidelines, rocked back on its heels and declared the document needed more work. *The New York Times* sadly observed that "[t]he backlash has some proponents of ethnic studies worried about losing momentum."[6]

What occasioned so much public discontent at a time when *diversity* is typically no more controversial than the wallpaper in a Holiday Inn?

The Ethnic Studies guidelines are (or perhaps were – this remains to be seen) an aggressive expansion of *diversity* in the state's K-12 curricula, but they are far from a beachhead. Apart from the guidelines, the California Department of Education's website already mentioned *diversity* some 3,420 times, and the Department had long established specialized statewide K-12 ventures such as the César E. Chávez model curriculum, which focused on the labor leader's life and work. In the very first sentence of the new *Ethnic Studies Model Curriculum* we are introduced to some of the neologisms of diversity-speak:

> *As early as the 1970s, some California public high schools began offering Ethnic Studies, positing that*

courses in the field would provide an opportunity to engage the hxrstory, cultures, contributions, perspectives, and experiences of groups that have been overlooked, hxrstorically marginalized, and often subjected to invisibility within mainstream courses.

"Hxrstory?" you might ask. A footnote explains:

Throughout this model curriculum, language is used that deliberately offers an alternative to traditional wording that could have a particular context within the dominant culture. More information about these terms can be found in the Glossary.

That glossary runs sixteen pages and includes surprising definitions of old words as well as new inventions. It also introduces tendentious political claims:

Boycott, Divestment, and Sanctions (BDS) is a global social movement that currently aims to establish freedom for Palestinians living under apartheid conditions.

"Capitalism" is presented in straight Marxist terms: "In a capitalist economy, surplus value (profit) is generated from human labor and everything is commodified."

"Cisheteropatriarchy" is helpfully unpacked as "a system of power that is based on the dominance of cisheterosexual men."

"'Nepantla' is a Náhuatl word [the language of the Aztecs] that was adopted by Chicanx writers, scholars, and feminists to describe an 'in-between space.' Chicana feminist, Gloria Anzaldua, was among the first to advance theorizing on the term, defining it as, a precarious space where transformation can occur. The term can be used to describe a variety of identity-related issues, including, race, gender, language, etc. Nepantla is the recognition of confusion, chaos, and messiness in one's understanding of self and the world. Nepantla also provides room for self-reflection to better understand and work through this liminal space."

"Race [is] a social construct created by European and American pseudo-scientists which sorts people by phenotype into global, social, and political hierarchies."

Oddly missing from the glossary is the word "diversity," perhaps because it is the ocean in which all these other words swim. *Diversity* is not missing from the model curriculum itself, which aims to "enable students to develop a deep appreciation for cultural diversity and inclusion, and aids in the eradication of bigotry, hate, and racism." The word grows like seaweed throughout the document. Students are encouraged to "celebrate the nation's wealth of diversity," which they learn how to do by playing "Diversity Bingo"; studying the "four core people of color groups" through the academic fields of "Black/African American Studies, Chicano/a Studies, Native American Studies, and Asian American Studies"; "learning the value and strength in diversity"; and discovering "the value of having a diverse citizenry."

Among the "general principles" in the Ethnic Studies Model Curriculum is that it:

Include information on the ethnic studies movement, specifically the Third World Liberation Front (TWLF),

*and its significance in the establishment of ethnic stud-
ies as a discipline and work in promoting diversity and
inclusion within higher education.*

For its transgressions against American history and civ-
ics, economics, and the English language, California's Ethnic Studies Model Curriculum deserves mockery. And it
received just that. Yet the committee that devised it is not
far from the mainstream of contemporary American K-12
education. It was just a little more candid about its inten-
tions than is usually the case.

Minoritized Voices

The University of South Dakota Law School counsels students as part of their orientation to consider whether they
are helping or hindering "minoritized voices." A helpful
flowchart guides the first-year law students to a judgment
that either "You're probably taking up space," or "You're
probably contributing to a space."

The participle "minoritized" is a fascinating word. It
seems to refer to the idea that some opinions are legitimately
black, legitimately Asian, etc., and that some opinions –
regardless of the ethnicity of those who hold them – are ille-
gitimate. This is what Congresswoman Ayanna Pressley
(D-Massachusetts) referred to on July 14, 2019, when she
spoke at the Netroots Nation conference:

*We don't need any more brown faces that don't want to
be a brown voice. We don't need black faces that don't
want to be a black voice. We don't need Muslims that*

don't want to be a Muslim voice. We don't need queers
that don't want to be a queer voice.

Pressley's declarations prompted some criticism, but what she said was perfectly in keeping with the current edicts of the *diversity* movement. Stick to your identity group and make sure everything you say fits with that identity group's prevailing ideology of the moment.

Promoters of *diversity* in its newest incarnation have to walk a careful line between "essentialism" and individualism. Essentialism is the idea that identity is fixed in nature. That would mean there is one and one only "black identity," and a set of views that comports with that identity. Powell's original *Bakke* opinion traded in racial essentialism. At the other end of the scale is the recognition that people really are individuals and may not care to have their opinions handed to them in a group identity basket. Pressley is less worried about essentialism than she is about an outbreak of individualism. A "brown face" that doesn't have a "brown voice" betrays group unity. Such a person is a race traitor.

But that odd phrase at the University of South Dakota Law School, "minoritized voices," is intended to ward off the sin of essentialism. The Law School doesn't care about making sure that the voices of people in minority groups are heard. Rather it wants "minoritized voices." What's the difference? Diversiphiles have been blogging about this for several years, so the answer is at hand. Someone named I. E. Smith (this appears to be a pen name), for example, writes in "Minority vs. Minoritized: Why the Noun Just Doesn't Cut It," that the noun "can be seen as dismissive," while the perfect passive participle correctly captures that groups are "social constructs" some of which "have less power or representation compared to other members or groups in society." These groups have been "minoritized." It's not their relative numbers that make a minority a minority, it's their exclusion from positions of power. The word "minoritized" is meant to fly free from the lurking suggestion that a minority group has any essential identity, and to emphasize instead that we are in the world of fluid identities vying for relative power. Smith explains, "People who are minoritized endure mistreatment."

This word play, of course, is a familiar part of the Left's Newspeak. Diversiphiles are in constant need of fresh euphemisms when they speak to the general public and new argot when they speak to their in-group. The old words are always at risk of becoming too clearly defined, exposing their contradictions and crude assumptions. *Diversity* itself has become one of those words increasingly troubled by excessive clarity. For a time, *diversity* could maintain two separate lives. On one hand, it reassured the white middle class that the goal was to overcome racial barriers. *Diversity* was the path to integration and to putting the old racial animosities behind us. On the other hand, *diversity* reassured blacks and other minority groups that it was a promise of access to social goods while maintaining group separatism. *Diversity* in this sense promised a new, socially advantageous form of segregation, and a path to reparations for past injustice.

These paths are not just separate, but divergent. How could one word, *diversity*, promise both? Only by sowing ambiguity. The word had to be kept free of exact definition. But as the public gradually caught on, new words had to be added. Today *diversity* is almost always doubled as "diversity and inclusion."

DIVERSITY IN COURT

Since I wrote *Diversity: The Invention of a Concept* more than fifteen years ago, I have kept moderately abreast of the topic. I followed the major court cases, principally *Grutter v. Bollinger* (2003); *Parents Involved in Community Schools v. Seattle School District No. 1* (2007); *Fisher v. the University of Texas* (2013 and 2016); and, most recently, *Students for Fair Admissions v. Harvard* (2018 and ongoing). *Grutter*, *Seattle*, and *Fisher* were important Supreme Court cases. *Fair Admissions* may well reach the Supreme Court, but as I write, the case is in the hands of United States District Court Judge Allison Burroughs. It is easy to get lost in the details of legal pleadings and court decisions, but for this short chronicle, these are the mountain peaks:

Grutter v. Bollinger. I began this account by invoking the moment on which Justice Sandra Day O'Connor bestowed the kiss of diversity on the nation, but a little more explanation is in order. This was a pair of cases. Barbara Grutter was an unsuccessful applicant to the University of Michigan Law School. Jennifer Gratz was an unsuccessful applicant to the University of Michigan undergraduate program. Lee Bollinger was the president of the University of Michigan. Grutter and Gratz, both white, sued the university for racial discrimination because they had been passed over in favor of significantly less qualified minority applicants. The university defended itself by asserting that its racial preferences existed to promote "diversity." It explained the good of diversity by saying it had provable educational benefits. Diversity supposedly helps students "learn better" and to become "active participants in our pluralistic, democratic society."

The U.S. Supreme Court struck down the University of Michigan's undergraduate racial preferences because they directly awarded admissions "points" on the basis of race. Jennifer Gratz won. But the Court decided that the Law School's use of racial preferences was acceptable because the Law School had pursued what it called "holistic assessment." This meant that instead of awarding points for racial minority status, the School blurred race into one indeterminate factor among many in admissions decisions. "Holistic assessment" was a transparent lie: the racial breakdown of the Law School's first-year classes was almost exactly the same year after year, just as if the School had applied a strict quota system. One of the dissenting Justices pointed this out, but the Supreme Court has a long tradition of turning a blind eye to useful deceptions.

In this case, Justice O'Connor found that, yes, the pursuit of "diversity" can be a compelling public interest sufficient to override Constitutional guarantees against racial discrimination, and, yes, the University of Michigan Law School's form of "holistic assessment" passes the Supreme Court's tests of "strict scrutiny," in that it was "narrowly tailored." Lee Bollinger and the University of Michigan won. Barbara Grutter lost. And Justice O'Connor also added her fanciful comment that she hoped that in twenty-five years, racial preference would no longer be necessary.

Actually, institutional arrangements that entail giant bureaucracies and cosseted interest groups seldom decide to call it a day and go home. And if anyone else ever suggests they should declare the work finished, the diversiphiles will fight as though someone had proposed putting Jefferson Davis on the dollar bill.

Parents Involved in Community Schools v. Seattle School District No. 1 was a case about how Seattle assigned students to popular high schools. The School District considered the race of applicants in trying to balance white and non-white enrollment. A non-profit group sued the District claiming that these preferences violated the Equal Protection clause of the Fourteenth Amendment and the Civil Rights Act of 1964. The U.S. Supreme Court ruled, consistent with *Grutter*, that, yes, *diversity* is a compelling public interest, but in a split decision, the majority of the Court ruled against the School District's racial balancing program. The Court decided this program was not "narrowly tailored" and was therefore illegal. Justice Roberts wrote the majority decision, demonstrating both his devotion to precedent (*Grutter*) and his skepticism about racial preferences. His opinion includes the now-famous line, "The way to stop discrimination on the basis of race is to stop discriminating on the basis of race."

Fisher v. Texas refers to a case that rose to the Supreme Court twice, in 2013 and again in 2016, usually referred to as *Fisher I* and *Fisher II*. Abigail Fisher was an unsuccessful applicant for undergraduate admission in 2008 to the University of Texas at Austin. The university had a double system that granted two kinds of racial preferences. One was a disguised racial preference system that granted admission to any student graduating in the top ten percent of his high school class. This meant that students from minority-dominated high schools who might not be especially academically talented could skip to the head of the line. But the university had other racial preferences as well.

In Fisher I, the Court decided that the Fifth Circuit had not held the university to the proper standard of strict scrutiny. It sent the case back to the Fifth Circuit with the demand that it apply the *Grutter* standard.

The best that can be said about what happened next is that the Fifth Circuit went through the motions. The University of Texas pretended to apply the strict scrutiny standards to itself and the Fifth Circuit pretended to believe the university. In Fisher II, the U.S. Supreme Court, in a 4–3 vote, pretended to believe them both. Justice Antonin Scalia memorably raised the "mismatch" concept, which is the idea that admitting underqualified students to a rigorous academic program ends up hurting the very students it is meant to advantage. In disproportionate numbers, such students end up at the bottom of their classes and generally underperforming their peers at less selective institutions. But Justice Scalia died in February 2016, four months before the Court handed down its decision.

Students for Fair Admissions v. Harvard is a case in which a group of Asian students are suing Harvard for racial discrimination because Harvard limits the number of Asians it will admit while it admits large numbers of black students who have nowhere near the academic qualifications of many of the Asian students who are rejected. Harvard has mounted the usual *diversity* defense, but the plaintiffs have brought to light documents that show chicanery on the part of the Harvard's admission officials. Harvard, for example, assigned low points to Asian applicants, sight unseen, for qualities of character such as "positive personality," likeability, courage, kindness, and being "widely respected."

Long experience has taught Americans not to expect anything in the way of straight talk about race from the nation's courts, and especially not the Supreme Court, unless you are willing to dig through the dissents. Justice Clarence Thomas in particular has a fine record of calling out the Court's catalogue of unconstitutional jurisprudence that has practically nullified the Equal Protection Clause. Respect for precedent has left the Court defending an ever-more preposterously elaborate *diversity* doctrine. That doctrine has the unfortunate flaw that it is educational nonsense. The color of a student's skin or the emotional energy he has invested in a racial identity makes no contribution to the quality of education on offer at a college or university, except when it becomes a psychological impediment, as in a so-called "stereotype threat," or other instances in which students invest in the belief that they are subject to invisible forms of discrimination. The Court's various rulings make such psychological impediments far more likely than they otherwise would be.

Liberal supporters of affirmative action are no happier with the Court's *diversity* doctrine than are conservative critics of racial preferences. Liberals would like a straight-forward policy of making up for past inequities by favoring present-day members of minority groups. Under the Court's *diversity* rules, the pursuit of equity is not a legitimate public policy reason for advantaging minority applicants. Conservatives want individuals to be treated as individuals on the basis of their merits. But under the *diversity* rules, individual merit is subordinated to group identity.

Though hardly anyone believes in the validity or pertinence of the Court's *diversity* distinctions, lawyers need to uphold the fiction and judges must act as if these distinctions make some kind of sense. *Diversity* jurisprudence is thus a game of make-believe.

HITTING THE BOOKS

Since writing *Diversity*, I have read what I take to be the most important scholarly books on the topic, and quite a few other kinds of *diversity* books: screeds on all sides of the issue, persistent pleas to admit students to college according to their class disadvantages or the locations of their high schools, and thunderous attacks on standardized testing. But my short list of the most worthwhile contributions is: Larry Purdy's *Getting Under the Skin of "Diversity"* (2008); Thomas Espenshade and Alexandria Radford's *No Longer Separate, Not Yet Equal* (2009); Russell Nieli's *Wounds That Will Not Heal* (2012); Richard Sander and Stuart Taylor, Jr.'s *Mismatch: How Affirmative Action Hurts Students It's Intended to Help, and Why Universities Won't Admit It* (2012); Tim Groseclose's *Cheating: An Insider's Report on the Use of Race in Admissions at UCLA* (2014); Gene Dattel's *Reckoning with Race* (2017); and Heather Mac Donald's *The Diversity Delusion* (2018). What all these books have in common is close attention to detail combined with a well-honed sense of the contradictory impulses that animate America's troubled efforts to figure out what to do about racial division.

Purdy's *Getting Under the Skin of "Diversity"* is a dismantling of one of the most famous justifications for racial preference, William Bowen and Derek Bok's *The Shape of the River* (1998). At the time of its publishing, Bowen was the former president of Princeton, and Bok the former president of Harvard. Purdy was the trial counsel to Grutter and Gratz in their Supreme Court cases. Purdy dismantles the *diversity* rationale piece by piece until there is nothing left but rhetorical rubble.[7]

Espenshade and Radford's *No Longer Separate, Not Yet Equal* is the faithful testimony of two liberal sociologists who would like very much to advance the American ideals of equality, but who are also careful truth-tellers. Their book is a tightly argued analysis of admissions data from eight universities, for the years 1983, 1993, and 1997. They had access to nearly a quarter of a million admissions records and supplemented this with their own survey of more than nine thousand students. The result is a book that is dense with statistics but always lucid. I turn to it again and again when I need to find authoritative data on how higher education's pursuit of *diversity* actually plays out. For example, long before Students for Fair Admissions filed its lawsuit against Harvard for discriminating against Asian students, Espenshade and Radford published compelling evidence of such discrimination as a settled pattern among elite institutions.

Their book is rich with admissions data, but it also examines how students "mix and mingle" on campus, how they perform academically, and how they shoulder the costs. The mix-and-mingle theme is a special interest of mine. In April 2019, the organization I lead, the National Association of Scholars, published two reports, *Neo-Segregation at Yale* and *Neo-Segregation at Wesleyan*, as part of a larger project we called "Separate but Equal, Again." The first author of both reports, Dion J. Pierre, spent time on these campuses interviewing students and gaining firsthand familiarity with how most mixing and mingling across racial and ethnic lines really happens. As our titles suggest, we found the barriers between groups to be formidable. Pierre traced this back to mistakes that the universities made in the 1960s when they attempted to appease unhappy black students by creating separate black-only programs and spaces.[8]

Espenshade and Radford touch on this gingerly. They observe the "increased propensity" of members of race or ethnic group "to develop ties with members of that group throughout one's college years." They find solace in that students do "interact" with other students outside their own group "though not as often as they interact with students who are more like themselves." How "often" is "often"? "Roughly 90 percent [of the 245,000 students in their study] report socializing frequently with, rooming with, and having as one of their five closest friends a classmate from the same racial or ethnic background."[9]

Nieli's *Wounds That Will Not Heal* is less about the details of how racial preferences work out in college life than it is about the controversies that racial preferences have ignited. Nieli casts his account as a "no-holds-barred critique of raced-based employment and university admissions policies, whose consequences for the social harmony and well-being of America, I believe, are almost wholly negative." But he overstates the no-holds-barred claim. The tone of *Wounds That Will Not Heal* is more meditative than excoriating, as Nieli walks us through the social science research. He tackles the so-called "contact hypothesis," (i.e. that putting people of different races together in college or a local community will demolish stereotypes and engender tolerance), the concept of "mismatch," ideas such as "stereotype vulnerability," the role of disincentives in undermining the academic performance of black students, and a great deal more. On the scale between indignation and disappointment over American public policies on race, Nieli is closer to disappointment.

Nieli's book connects with Purdy's *Getting Under the Skin of "Diversity"* in an important way. With lawyerly precision, Purdy refutes the bible of diversity rationales, Bowen and Bok's *Shape of the River*. Nieli, citing Purdy, covers some of the same water, but adds refutations to two sequels to Bowen and Bok's book. The Andrew W. Mellon Foundation, headed at the time by William Bowen, sponsored *The Shape of the River* (1998) and then went further into the water in the edited volumes *The Source of the River* (2003) and *The Taming of the River* (2009).[10] Nieli comes up with the genial phrase "River Pilots" for the collection of diversiphiles whose rationalizations of racial preference fill up these studies, which he refers to as Rivers I, II, and III. River I, of course, is the statistically convoluted claim that the beneficiaries of racial preferences genuinely benefit from all the special treatment they receive. Harvard and other elite universities are helping to build a new class of elite black professionals.

River II and III are much less sanguine. Nieli writes: "In River II the authors do get candid and acknowledge that it may not be in the power of college administrators to do much about negative stigma and the imputation of inferiority to groups receiving special admissions preferences." In some places the River Pilots try to argue against their own findings, but in River III it emerges that it is the students' "classmates, not college officials or faculties who set the general tone and determine the nature of racial atmosphere on campus." And "the most frequent source of derogatory comments was other students."[11]

Nieli's own judgment is that the River Pilots misdiagnose what lies behind the hardships that these preferenced students often encounter. He writes, "The results of such segregation and isolation clearly depend on the internal strengths and weaknesses of the group involved, something the River Pilots, with their apologetic and exculpatory purpose, refuse to acknowledge."[12] He contrasts the experiences of Chinese and Vietnamese students, who are often similarly isolated, with the experiences of black students in elite institutions.

Sander and Taylor, Jr.'s *Mismatch* (2012) was published the same year as Nieli's *Wounds*, and Nieli cites Sander's earlier work on how poorly law students admitted via racial preference perform in their academic programs. That the mismatch concept has become part of the common vocabulary of *diversity* critics is testimony to the power of Sander and Taylor's analysis and the vigor of their writing. Sander has spent years waging legal battles to obtain further data that bears on his "hypothesis," but *Mismatch* isn't spare on detail. They recount at one point that George Mason University Law School broke with the almost universal pattern of preferencing black applicants: "In 1995 black applicants had been about eight times as likely to be admitted as whites with comparable credentials." But by 1999, the preferences were almost entirely gone.

Unfortunately, so were many of the black students who

were "fully competitive" and could have been admitted on their own academic merit. What happened, Sander and Taylor explain, was a "preference cascade." The black students who were a good match for George Mason University Law School were admitted to and chose to attend "more elite schools" for which they were underqualified. In light of this, the law school snapped back to using racial preferences in its admissions – a policy that was strongly encouraged by the American Bar Association.[13]

One of the profound lessons of *Mismatch* is that the system is rigged. A college or university that tries to escape the regime of racial preferences faces not just the vituperation of preference supporters, but also a loss in competition for qualified students and pressure from accreditors. There is no easy way out.

Groseclose's *Cheating* (2014) is a whistleblower's account of how the University of California, Los Angeles deliberately and persistently broke the law to engage in race-preferential admissions. Groseclose was a professor of political science and economics at UCLA who was asked to serve on a faculty committee overseeing admissions. During his term on the committee, the UCLA Chancellor, Norm Abrams, paid a visit and told the committee that he wanted it to switch procedures "to make the whole admissions process holistic." Remember: this is the magic word that the University of Michigan Law School used to persuade Justice O'Connor in the *Grutter* case to wink at the school's flagrant racial quotas. Chancellor Abrams enunciated his enthusiasm for the "holistic" in 2006, a decade after the State of California passed Proposition 209, the referendum that outlawed racial preferences.[14]

Apparently, when racial preferences are outlawed, only outlaws have racial preferences, and the greatest outlaws in California are college administrators. In one year – from 2006 to 2007, "the number of African Americans enrolled" in UCLA freshman class neatly doubled – "from 102 in 2006 to 204 in 2007."

Grossclose, who is a statistically literate professor, began to pay closer attention to how UCLA was conducting admissions. In Spring 2008, he asked the Admissions Director for a random sample of one thousand applications so that he could perform a statistical analysis. The Admissions Director deflected him by saying the whole committee could do the analysis, and then by angrily confronting him in a meeting," asking "Why do you want the data? What do you want to examine?"

This story is recounted in the opening pages of *Cheating*, and what follows is an edge-of-the-chair account of UCLA's skullduggery in trying to hide its misfeasance, while Grossclose zeroes in on the facts. *Cheating* is a celebrated first-person account of how *diversity* really plays out behind the closed doors of university administrators' offices. Professor Sander plays a key role in the story. In the end, Grossclose decamps from UCLA to join the Economics Department at George Mason University – where, as Sander has instructed us, the *diversity* game is also afoot.

Dattel's *Reckoning with Race* (2017), unlike these other books, is not primarily about higher education. It is a general history of race in America from 1800 to the present, emphasizing the differences between the North and the South. Dattel's start date bears attention, as *The New York Times* has recently launched a campaign to make the year

1619 – the year the first African slaves were supposedly brought to America – the true founding of our society.[15] The claim about the year is false, African slaves having been transported to the Eastern seaboard long before 1619, but the "1619 Project" will almost certainly succeed with school teachers, textbook writers, and liberal pundits as one more welcome way to denigrate America. The existence of slavery in Africa itself and through most of human history, including in pre-colonial Native America, won't stand in the way of a new mythology.

Dattel's book is aimed at several kinds of de-mythologizing. A major theme is the racial hypocrisy of the North. Dattel is also keen to document the undercurrent of ethnic antagonisms that have been endemic to American society. The subtitle of his book is "America's Failure," but in contrast to *The New York Times*, Dattel seems to be calling out a specific failure rather than condemning America comprehensively. There is a difference. Dattel isn't sour on the nation's possibilities. He locates those squarely in education. He writes: "Education is the prerequisite for intellectual, physical, and economic mobility. It is portable, flexible, and the basis of individual and group self-esteem and confidence."[16]

This leads him to take what are surely controversial positions, as when he quotes a black mother in Manhattan who is worried that "her child's school would 'turn all white.'" He observes, "The segregation issue is not entirely one-sided, for blacks, too, have concerns – about the percentage of white students in a class." In this vein, he questions "diversity for diversity's sake," as a replacement for "merit-based tests." *Diversity*, as it happens, leads off in unexpected directions as when the Supreme Court ruled in 1992 in *Ayres v.*

Fordice that Mississippi had underfunded three historically black universities by $500 million. But to claim the funds, the three universities had to achieve "10 percent other-race enrollment." They sought to do this by offering "diversity scholarships" to white students.[17] Dattel's book is a goldmine of such material, and beyond the book itself, his knowledge of the racial bargaining practices at Yale proved invaluable to Pierre and me in our study of neo-segregation.

The last (and most recent) work on my short list of the most important recent scholarly books on diversity is Heather Mac Donald's *Diversity Delusion* (2018). Mac Donald is among America's sharpest social critics, a Mencken for our times, and we are fortunate that she has devoted some of her attention to higher education, and some to *diversity*'s non-campus exurbs. This book is divided into parts, including race, gender, and bureaucracy, as well as one titled "The Purpose of the University." In her introduction to the volume, Mac Donald delivers one swift verdict: "'Diversity' in the academy is purported to be about bridge-building and broadening people's experiences. It has had the opposite effect: dividing society, reducing learning, and creating an oppositional mind-set that prevents individuals from seizing the opportunities available to them."[18]

Apart from her precise and accurate summation, Mac Donald has an unsurpassed eye for details. She is especially good in catching the way diversiphiles speak. A French professor attempts to excuse violent protesters at Berkeley by saying they attacked property *very sparingly, destroying just enough*" to get an event cancelled.[19] President Salovey at Yale "issued the usual fawning declarations of sorrow for the tribulations experienced by Yale's minority students."

The wind chimes of Salovey's ersatz sorrow come across as he explains, "In my thirty-five years on this campus, I have never been as simultaneously moved, challenged, and encouraged by our community – and all the promise it embodies – as in the past two weeks." He is referring to the period of racial blustering and intimidation that continued for weeks after the infamous mobbing of Professor Christakis by students upset that his wife had defended the freedom of students to choose their own Halloween costumes.

I'll refrain from quoting more of Mac Donald's *Diversity Delusion* on the grounds that I might not have much of my own to say afterwards, so right Mac Donald is on topics such as the contempt that university elites feel for the public's aversion to affirmative action, the adverse consequences of racial preferences for the preferees, and the farcical – her word – idea of "microaggressions."

Having piled up seven books for the reader's nightstand, I can think of many others that deserve attention. But these seven are enough to conjure the intellectual heft of the criticism of the diversity movement that has arisen since Justice O'Conner puckered up and bestowed the Supreme Court's kiss on Powell's peculiar idea.

CLIPPED

Over the years I've also continuously clipped and filed away articles on *diversity*, so that I would be equipped if ever the need arose to explain in day-by-day, week-by-week chronology how this idea slowly faded from the cutting-edge to the banality of a postage stamp slogan. Now that I am actually writing a coda to the book, the files seem of faded interest.

At first glance they testify mostly to how commonplace the term became and how trivial were many of its applications.

The potential for banality was, of course, part of *diversity*'s appeal from the beginning. The ubiquitous command "Celebrate Diversity!" offered an easy absolution for the frictions that arise among people, as though they could be wished away in a sudden outpouring of relativism.

They can't. The animus between Islamists on one hand and Jews and Christians on the other is unlikely to evaporate the moment someone's eyes fall on a "Coexist" bumper sticker. The discomfort that many heterosexuals feel around gays – the attitude that gays register as homophobia – might be silenced by the *diversity* edict but it lingers. Feminists are fracturing over how far the embrace of *diversity* must extend. Many who have been lecturing the world for generations that "gender is a social construct" are now confronted with men pretending to be women who seek to compete in women's sports and use women's locker rooms. Does the god of *diversity* require that "transgendered" individuals who are genetically and often anatomically male be accepted as real women in these situations?

The *diversity* movement has evolved in other still more strident ways. Instead of beckoning Americans of all sorts to a benevolent group hug, it now seems to demand a hard division between those who have enjoyed "white privilege" and those who have supposedly been given the short end of the stick. *Diversity* now accommodates a free-floating accusation of "white supremacy" that is intended to indict 72.4 percent of the population.

"Celebrate diversity" has not gone away as a slogan or a cultural meme. The banal idea of *diversity* is still in play in schools and churches, but it has been losing ground to more belligerent forms of the idea, often signaled with the new phrase "diversity and inclusion." *Inclusion* is a demand that the prevailing standards, whatever they were, must make way for the cultural preferences of the newly arrived. When I wrote about this in 2003, I pointed out that affirmative action was a call for an integrated society, but the demand for inclusion rejects the ideal of integration and insists that differences must be accepted on their own terms.

At the time, diversiphiles were divided about the goal. Some still sought social unity founded on broad tolerance. But that faction has now lost decisively to others whose goal is permanent division and the elevation of group differences as the highest good. The word "inclusion" is tossed in by diversiphiles as a diversionary tactic. No one wants to come right out to say, "Division is what we want." But it is.

Do my files of press clippings illuminate this transition? One thing they illuminate for sure is that the concept of diversity became pervasive. By way of illustration, here are seven articles pulled at random from my 2014 file. The first is a *New York Times* review of an exhibition held at the Institute for the Study of the Ancient World, which featured objects from the Ptolemaic period of Egypt, 232 BC–30 BC. The review, titled "Multiculturalism: Nothing New," focuses on the "diversity of cultures" in Ptolemaic Egypt. True enough that Egypt at the time was a crossroads of cultures, but is this the most important thing we can take from this epoch and its art? Or was the idea of cultural diversity so mesmerizing that the reviewer couldn't see anything else?[20]

Then there's the clipping from the journal *Science* extolling "Scientific Diversity Interventions." The article's six authors bemoan the slow pace at which "representation of women and racial and ethnic minorities has increased in recent decades," and propose to accelerate it by new "diversity interventions." These interventions will overcome "implicit biases" by using "evidence-based" techniques for "improved diversity-promoting behavior." The awkward language no doubt is intended to underscore the scientific seriousness of this vapid demand for quotas.[21]

Next is a story from the business pages of *The New York Times*, "Not Walking the Walk on Board Diversity," which chastises the footwear company Skechers USA for promising in 2011 to increase the number of women and minorities on its board and then failing to do so. Skechers, oddly enough, said its "primary focus is on maximizing shareholder value."[22]

Further in the pile is an op-ed, "The Diversity of Islam," and a short report in *The Wall Street Journal*, "Study Finds Diversity Toll." The latter discusses a University of Colorado study that purported to show that "women and nonwhite executives who push for women and nonwhites to be hired and promoted suffer when it comes to their own performance reviews." An article from *Diverse Education* calls on historically black colleges and universities to improve their diversity efforts by "tending to the needs of lesbian, gay, bisexual and transgendered students." Yet another article from the *Times* reports the city comptroller had called for New York to do a better job promoting the "diversity of its vendors."[23]

Enough of that. Can we can make anything of the jumble? We find *diversity* invoked to explain ancient art, to demand more positions for women and minorities in the hard sciences, to shame for-profit businesses to appoint more women and minorities to their boards, to extoll the virtues of Islam, to warn women and minorities against favoring own-group hires, to pressure HBCUs to be more gay friendly, and to elbow city bureaucrats to throw more business to minority vendors.

A simple translation is that by 2014 *diversity* was an all-purpose "I want" word, especially useful to advancing the claims of women and ethnic minorities, but with some spill-over to sexual minorities. None of the authors feel a need to explain what *diversity* is or why promoting it is good. The one article suggesting a negative dimension indirectly testifies that *diversity* has long since been established as self-replicating within the corporate world. *Diverse* executives will favor in-group hires, even at some danger to their own advancement.

We are, in other words, in a world where *diversity* is a social norm, not a frontier. But it is not so well established a social norm that it goes without saying. Far from it. The word is evoked again, again, and again, and always somewhere between a righteous demand and a cheer. We can have a little more respect for Ptolemaic Egypt or Islam knowing that they, too, embrace *diversity*.

OBAMA'S DIVERSITY

My exercise in pulling out some old clippings wasn't entirely arbitrary. I picked a year in the midst of Barack Obama's presidency – perhaps the most uneventful year. He had been re-elected in 2012, but dissatisfactions with his policies were mounting to the point where the Republicans took control of the Senate in November 2014. Republicans already controlled the House. After November, the Republican majority was the largest it had been since 1929–31. A Democratic president in this situation had little room for legislative maneuver, and President Obama in particular was not suited by temperament to work constructively with an opposition party. He governed mostly by regulatory fiat and international diplomacy.[24] In many ways he was a figurehead president.[25]

As the first black president of the United States, Obama can be considered the personal fulfillment of the *diversity* doctrine. He brought to the presidency little record of political accomplishment or achievement in other walks of life. He was a handsome, well-spoken man known for his leftist allies and opaque background. Born from a short-lived marriage between his white mid-western mother and his black Kenyan father, he lived in Indonesia from age six to ten with his mother and his Indonesian step-father. At ten, he moved to Hawaii to be raised by his grandparents, who sent him to an elite private school.

Although Obama himself published two memoirs of his early years, and although several researchers and biographers have dug more deeply into his past, Obama's beginnings remain surprisingly faint.[26] He is a man who doesn't seem to be from a particular place, although he does in fact have roots of a sort in Hawaii. Moreover, his family was also unsettled and footless. His earliest substantial connection with anyone outside his family appears to have been with the communist drifter Frank Marshall Davis. This detail is more perplexing than enlightening.

The vagueness of Obama's beginnings is repeated in his adolescence and early manhood. In one sense we know very little about his college years, except for his involvement with the Democratic Socialists of America and with left-wing activist groups at Occidental College and Columbia University. But in another sense, we know a lot.

David Garrow's massive biography, *Rising Star: The Making of Barack Obama*, published after Obama left office, unrolls a vast amount of new detail, though much of it is trivial and hardly any of it defines Obama's character in a positive way. We learn from Garrow, for example, that Obama spent Sunday, January 24, 1982, watching the Super Bowl with his friends Ron and Phil at 11 Cranberry Street in Brooklyn Heights. The fact seems to have no bearing on anything other than the mundaneness of his existence at the time. But Garrow also recounts Obama's uneven embrace of radical politics. We learn, for example, that Obama "exaggerated his involvement" with the anti-apartheid divestment movement at Columbia University in 1983.[27]

And Garrow gives us glimpses of Obama's aloof and occasionally cruel personality. We hear of one girlfriend who took offence at "all the artifice in his manner." We witness his casual cruelty to his girlfriend at Occidental, Alex McNear, to whom he acknowledges, "you are correct when you say that initially you were to me nothing more than a lovely wraith I had shaped to fit my needs." He accuses Alex at one point of distinguishing too much between mind and body, which he criticizes as "a vestige of western thought."[28]

It seems the more we know about Obama in this period, the less accessible he becomes. He writes to Alex, "I play with words and work pretty patterns in my head, but the hole is dark and deep below, immeasurably deep. Know that it is always there, rats nibbling at the foundation, and it can set me to tremble." In another letter he confesses, "I am often cruel, and my mind will flash on screen scenes of violence or petty malevolence or betrayal on my part." This seems more like a character out of an Edgar Allan Poe story or a Dostoevsky novel than a man destined for the White House, but it fits with his transition to full-time political actor. Obama was an empty space onto which could be projected all manner of other people's dreams.[29]

His years in Chicago after he graduated from Harvard Law School are marked by his dabbling further in radical politics and becoming a "community organizer" – itself an occupation outside the usual range of jobs in American labor markets.

All of this obscurity, compounded with his own lack of candor, would normally put someone like Obama too far outside the mainstream to be taken seriously as a political figure. Obscurity, of course, can be an asset if it comes with a plausibly heroic story. Abraham Lincoln the rail-splitter came out of nowhere, but his obscure origins were filled in with a powerful narrative of a man determined to rise above his humble beginnings. Obama's origin, by contrast, seems more privileged than humble. From his elite private school, he went to Occidental College then transferred to Columbia University. He was soon admitted to Harvard Law School, where he served as an editor of the *Harvard Law Review*. Nothing in the story suggests hardship or struggle except Obama's own account of missing his father, whom he met only briefly in 1971.

Whatever drawbacks this history might have had for a pre-*diversity* presidential candidate were wiped away by the *diversity* doctrine. The vagueness of his identity made Obama a template for *diversity* itself. He could represent a victim category – black Americans – without the scars of actual victimhood and without the weight of a narrative that placed him much of anywhere on the American social map. He was an everyman, or at least an everywhere *diversity* man, crowned with victimhood without the encumbrance of tragedy. His natural speaking voice was that of a "white American" and his cultural reflexes were those of someone raised in "white America," but he had learned through substantial effort to perform some amount of "blackness." The black community respected this. He wasn't a black trying to "act white." He was a man deciding to honor a portion of his heritage by learning to be black – but not too black.

The *diversity* doctrine offers very little to impoverished blacks in communities beset with violence, drugs, lawlessness of all sorts, poor educational opportunities, and the breakdown of the two-parent family. *Diversity* is instead a gift to the upwardly mobile black middle class, for whom it means preferential college admissions, scholarships, and career opportunities. These gifts can and often do have unintended negative consequences, but in the world of black professional parents, the *diversity* doctrine is embraced as just compensation for all the obstacles black Americans have endured and overcome.

Obama was the perfected image of the aspiring, upwardly mobile black man who, better yet, had remained devoted to the black community as a whole. His work as a community organizer and a member of a black church in Chicago epitomized him as someone who "remembered" and was not interested solely in his own advancement.

These are all matters of image and reputation. On a closer look, they dissolve into insubstantial gestures – but then *diversity* almost always melts away like that. Large claims turn out to be based on small facts or no facts at all. What's wanted is the photogenic figure who can represent aspiration unencumbered by the ballast of hard living. Obama is the man without college grades; the man who voted "present" when a bill up before a legislative house demanded a yes or a no; the man who regularly attended Chicago's Trinity United Church of Christ but never once heard its pastor, the fiery Reverend Jeremiah Wright, damn America.

President Obama carried this immunity all the way through his White House years. *Diversity*, as our national make-believe doctrine of recovered innocence, had found its man.

His presidency represented three aspects of the *diversity* doctrine. First, Obama stood as an exemplar of black pride to almost the whole black community, poor and prosperous alike. The force of group solidarity is a basic ingredient of *diversity*, and Obama's lack of specific location within the black community made it much easier for him to stand as a symbol of the whole.

Second, Obama was fluent in the language and symbols of diversiphiles and could thus represent the ideology of aspiration in the black middle class. This identification differs from general solidarity with the black community as a whole. It is the coded speech in which members of a privileged group acknowledge one another. Obama's message in this channel was one of moderation: he understood how to advance the *diversity* agenda quietly and without overt risk of arousing a backlash. In this he almost succeeded. His second-term policy initiative that went under the title "Affirmatively Furthering Fair Housing" (AFFH) was a plan that would have forced most of the nation's suburbs into submission to Democrat-controlled city governments, as a step towards the radical diminishment of the political power of the white middle class and the capture of its tax base to fund inner city constituencies. (Technically, AFFH was a provision of the 1868 Fair Housing Act. Obama tried to use it to assert federal control over local governments, turning suburbs, as one critic put it, "into helpless satellites of nearby megacities."[30] The leverage was to withhold HUD grants until the local governments agreed to build high-density low-income housing under federal administration.) The mainstream press paid virtually no attention to Affirmatively Furthering Fair Housing, though it was called out by conservatives such as Stanley Kurtz.[31] Had Hillary Clinton won the 2016 presidential election, Obama's redistribution-ist plan would no doubt have moved forward. *Diversity* was from the start a soft sell for economic redistribution and transfer of political power. Obama's mastery of this soft sell earned him ardent support among those who stood most to gain by such transfers.

Third, Obama perfected the appeal to white diversiphiles. His debut on the national stage as the keynote speaker at the Democratic National Convention in 2004 began by his invoking the idea that "my presence on this stage is pretty unlikely." He mentions his Kenyan father who "grew up herding goats," but found "a scholarship to study in a magical place, America, that shone as a beacon of freedom and opportunity to so many who had come before." In other words, Obama first appeared before Americans as a beneficiary of America's generosity and hospitality: the positive side of *diversity*.

A few sentences later, he mentions the word explicitly, saying that he is "grateful for the diversity of my heritage" and knows that "my story is part of the larger American story." Diversity is thus quietly inserted into the idea of "the American dream," which becomes the main theme of the sixteen-minute speech. In its final movement, Obama invokes national unity: "E pluribus unum. Out of many, one." He attacks the unnamed villains "who are preparing to divide us, the spin masters, the negative ad peddlers who embrace the politics of anything goes." And he answers these phantoms with the most famous lines of his career: "Well, I say to them tonight, there is not a liberal America and a conservative America – there is the United States of America. There is not a Black America and a White America and Latino America and Asian America – there's the United States of America."[32]

The speech vaulted Obama into national prominence and laid the groundwork for his successful 2008 presidential campaign, in which he was still able to pose successfully as a man who transcended racial division. Eventually, this image became pretty threadbare. John Gabriel, the editor of the online magazine *Ricochet*, mocked Obama in November 2014, writing in what became a widely repeated tagline: "My favorite part about the Obama era is all the racial healing."[33] By then, Obama had shown his hand too often in aggravating racial division within the country, but he held to the pose as a racial healer as long as he could.

In his 2008 campaign for the Democratic nomination he gave several speeches emphasizing his commitment to racial healing, including his March 18 address at the National Constitution Center in Philadelphia, where he answered critics who had pointed out his long-term association with the virulently anti-white Reverend Jeremiah Wright. Obama's answer is worth quoting at length for the light it casts on the ambiguities that make up so much of his appeal to white diversiphiles:

And yet, it has only been in the last couple of weeks that the discussion of race in this campaign has taken a particularly divisive turn.

On one end of the spectrum, we've heard the implication that my candidacy is somehow an exercise in affirmative action; that it's based solely on the desire of wide-eyed liberals to purchase racial reconciliation on the cheap. On the other end, we've heard my former pastor, Reverend Jeremiah Wright, use incendiary language to express views that have the potential not only to widen the racial divide, but views that denigrate both the greatness and the goodness of our nation; that rightly offend white and black alike.

I have already condemned, in unequivocal terms, the statements of Reverend Wright that have caused such controversy. For some, nagging questions remain. Did I know him to be an occasionally fierce critic of American domestic and foreign policy? Of course. Did I ever hear him make remarks that could be considered controversial while I sat in church? Yes. Did I strongly disagree with many of his political views? Absolutely – just as I'm sure many of you have heard remarks from your pastors, priests, or rabbis with which you strongly disagreed.

But the remarks that have caused this recent

firestorm weren't simply controversial. They weren't simply a religious leader's effort to speak out against perceived injustice. Instead, they expressed a profoundly distorted view of this country – a view that sees white racism as endemic, and that elevates what is wrong with America above all that we know is right with America; a view that sees the conflicts in the Middle East as rooted primarily in the actions of stalwart allies like Israel, instead of emanating from the perverse and hateful ideologies of radical Islam.

As such, Reverend Wright's comments were not only wrong but divisive, divisive at a time when we need unity; racially charged at a time when we need to come together to solve a set of monumental problems – two wars, a terrorist threat, a falling economy, a chronic health care crisis and potentially devastating climate change; problems that are neither black or white or Latino or Asian, but rather problems that confront us all.

Given my background, my politics, and my professed values and ideals, there will no doubt be those for whom my statements of condemnation are not enough. Why associate myself with Reverend Wright in the first place, they may ask? Why not join another church? And I confess that if all that I knew of Reverend Wright were the snippets of those sermons that have run in an endless loop on the television and YouTube, or if Trinity United Church of Christ conformed to the caricatures being peddled by some commentators, there is no doubt that I would react in much the same way.

But the truth is, that isn't all that I know of the man. The man I met more than twenty years ago is a man who helped introduce me to my Christian faith, a man who spoke to me about our obligations to love one another; to care for the sick and lift up the poor. He is a man who served his country as a U.S. Marine; who has studied and lectured at some of the finest universities and seminaries in the country, and who for over thirty years led a church that serves the community by doing God's work here on Earth – by housing the homeless, ministering to the needy, providing day care services and scholarships and prison ministries, and reaching out to those suffering from HIV/AIDS.[34]

I read the negation with which this begins as an acknowledgement of a truth that he needs to exorcize: "the implication that my candidacy is somehow an exercise in affirmative action; that it's based solely on the desire of wide-eyed liberals to purchase racial reconciliation on the cheap." His evasive and self-exculpatory account of this relation with Reverend Wright is his own effort to purchase something on the cheap. He wants to keep the credibility within the black community of having been a member of a black nationalist, white-hating church, while brushing off all the racist, factional, and hate-filled entailments of that association.

The speech, of course, succeeded, not least because his white supporters were cast in the role of giving him absolution, and thus reassuring themselves of their own diversiphilic generosity.

The three components of Obama's diversity persona – his generalized identification with the black community as a whole, his commitment to a hard-edged insider's game of diversity politics aimed at appealing to the black diversiphile elite, and his racial reconciliation "on the cheap" to white liberals – were in uneasy balance. Eventually, he settled on the second as his primary theme, but he never entirely abandoned attempts to play the other two strings when he needed them.

IDENTITY

Audrey Hall, an eleven-year-old from the Bronx, recently won a New York Public Library summer reading essay contest. Audrey reviewed *Blended*, a story about a mixed-race girl of divorced parents – as Audrey writes, "a mixed girl, like me!!"

Audrey is worldly for her eleven years. She foresees that she will have to check the "Other" Box for her "Ethnic Identification" when she applies for jobs or has "paper work." But she has a keen sense of who she is: "I am a true New Yorker born in the Bronx, Italian from my Mom's side of my family and Jamaican from my dad's side of my family. Like Isabella from the book my hair is curly, crazy and uncontrollable!"[35]

The critic Kevin Williamson responded to Audrey in a gentle essay in *National Review*, in which he invokes his own background as an adoptee who grew up in small city in Texas. Like Audrey, he was drawn to libraries at a young age but he slides from that shared interest to a contrast. What the very young Kevin Williamson discovered in books were "things you have in common with people ... are a lot more complicated and important than what your parents are like or where you live." Williamson is attempting to coax Audrey away from her focus on herself to look at the larger world. He writes, "There was a famous playwright in ancient Rome named Terence, who wrote: 'I am human, and I think nothing human is alien to me.'"[36]

Terence may be a little over Audrey's head right now, but she may someday come to realize what big-hearted, wise advice it is. Williamson has offered her a way out of the thicket of self-centered, group identitarianism.

Every child in the world has to master elements of social identity. Almost always this means learning one's place in a family and, step by step, encountering the members of a wider circle of kin. Along with this comes some understanding of the people who are nearby but are not relatives: the immediate community. Then begin the complications. Gaining a sense of the world with yourself at the center – the egocentric view of the universe – has eventually to make room for aspects of identity that are external facts. Part of what it means to be Audrey from the Bronx is that she isn't from Queens or Brooklyn. Audrey has already realized she doesn't have any say in what labels are fixed to those "boxes" of ethnic identification. But she has considerable say over how important she is going to make them in her own life.

Audrey is far from alone in being lured at any early age into the ideology of diversity. As the commentator Joy Pullman points out, the world's largest publisher of books for school-age children – Scholastic – has a 2019 back-to-school catalogue for grades three to six which is entirely devoted to identity politics. Scholastic partnered with a group called "We Need Diverse Books" to promote tales such as *Amina's Voice* ("After her family's mosque is attacked, Amina must choose: hide who she really is ... or speak up, sing out, and be heard."); *Mascot* ("Noah may be stuck in a wheelchair after his accident, but he's not about to live life on the sidelines."); and *The Unwanted: Stories of Syrian Refugees.* As Pullman describes Scholastic's project, "The end goal of all of this is also extremely clear: fomenting the rise of identity politics among increasingly younger children, to saturate everyone's families, schools, and public squares with far-left and hugely divisive politics."[37]

Identity is never trivial. As an anthropologist, I've spent most of my intellectual career wrestling with the multitude of ways that different cultures pose basic questions of identity and their more complicated follow-ons. What does it mean to belong to a tribe or a clan within a tribe? Is a modern nation, as one anthropologist famously put it, just an "imagined community?" Or is it, in some deeper sense, real? What does it mean to belong to a "generation," as in the Greatest, Baby Boomer, X, or Millennial generations? Are we citizens of the country in which we hold formal citizenship or are we "citizens of the world?" Ethnic boundaries are seldom fixed once and for all. Who gets to cross them, and how?

In America today some of these questions have become especially vexed. The "group identity" that someone lays claim to sometimes seems to eclipse everything else that might distinguish an individual. Or at least other attainments are subordinated: a man might identify himself not as a lawyer, but as a Black lawyer, or a Hispanic lawyer. We can never know in advance how seriously to take such self-labeling. It could be a small concession to the *diversity* consciousness of our times, but often it is a signal of a deeper sense of group identification. When we lead with an ethnic qualifier, or some other group identifier that implies a history of victimization (woman, gay, Muslim, undocumented, etc.) we are already several steps inside the world of identitarian thinking.

Group identity is not just a matter of where we place ourselves, but of how willing we are to be policed by others who speak "for" the group. Groups claim group interests, and they guard their boundaries. Elizabeth Warren claimed Cherokee ancestry, but the Cherokee Nation rejected her claim.[38] Rachel Dolezal presented herself as an American black and persuaded enough others of this to serve as president of the Spokane chapter of the NAACP for a year (2014–15). When it was discovered that she had no African ancestry, the NAACP issued a statement supporting her, but a petition was circulated calling for her removal from the position. A great deal of public controversy ensued, leading to her resignation.[39]

Group identity, above all, can be deployed as a weapon. In the fall of 2015, a black student at the University of Missouri (Mizzou) claimed that a driver had yelled a racial epithet at him, which set off a cascade of racial grievance claims that led the university's football team to declare that it would not take the field again until the university system president, Tim Wolfe, resigned.[40] The black students organized as "Concerned Student 1950" and issued a list of demands.[41] The president and the chancellor both resigned as accusations of racism against the university reached a crescendo. Word of this successful action fueled black activist groups on many other campuses, most of them already primed by the Black Lives Matter coalition. Formed in the wake of the 2013 acquittal of George Zimmerman in the death of Trayvon Martin, Black Lives Matter protests gained in intensity after the deaths in 2014 of Michael Brown and Eric Garner.

None of this protest bore specifically on higher education, but by the time of the Mizzou protests, recrimination against colleges and universities emerged as a major focus. A favored technique, following the Concerned Student 1950 model, was the issuing by organized groups of black students of lists of demands. A group calling itself "WeThe-Protesters" compiled eighty of these lists onto a single gateway website, "The Demands."[42]

The demands almost always included the imposition of "diversity requirements" on all students, the hiring of more "diverse" faculty members, and the sharp reduction of emphasis on the ideas and writings of "dead white men." Most college and university presidents who were faced with these protests, and the accompanying tactics of occupying administrative offices, promptly appeased the protesters with a combination of money and promises.

That is a story worth telling in its own right, but I bring it up here only to underscore that identity politics coalesces around group grievance. It musters and then intensifies the anger of those who see themselves in the mirror of racial injustice – or such other injustices as form the mythos of group unity.

None of this is to deny the reality of those injustices, at least those that comprise the terrible history of the oppression of blacks in America. The reality of today's injustices, however, poses harder questions. In a fair number of cases, claims about racial assaults, verbal attacks, and vandalism have turned out to be spurious. A category of "fake crimes" has arisen, typically in the form of acts in which the "victim" who comes forward with a complaint is discovered to be the perpetrator. Jussie Smollett's exploit in January 2019, in which he hired two Nigerian brothers to assist him in staging a fake racial attack on himself, epitomizes the genre. Dozens, perhaps hundreds, of campus incidents involving nooses, anonymous notes on doors, and drive-by epithets are the Smollett-ization of group grievance in higher education. But to be fair to Jussie, he just made more visible a tactic that had been practiced and perfected on campus by enterprising students for many years before he tried it out on the street of Chicago. Race is frequently at the center of these claims, but sex, gender, and other group markers come into play as well.[43]

The marshalling of group identity as a way to gain relative privilege is the theme of two studies I mentioned earlier, *Neo-Segregation at Yale* and *Neo-Segregation at Wesleyan*, in which Dion Pierre and I trace the origins of racial self-separation on campus back to the 1960s, when college presidents such as Yale's Kingman Brewster were desperate to admit much larger cohorts of black students. Large percentages of the black students admitted to places such as Yale and Wesleyan failed in their first year. Most of the remaining black students organized themselves into groups that spurned their college's integrationist ethos. They appealed instead to the black nationalism of figures such as Malcolm X and later, the Black Panthers.[44]

These foundational moves towards aggressive identity politics preceded Justice Powell's enunciation of the *diversity* doctrine by about fifteen years. *Diversity* and the expression of ethnic exclusion are plainly not one and the same thing, but they eventually fused. Today, the loudest demands for *diversity* have no echo at all of Kingman Brewster's fond hope for racial integration. *Diversity* is now a prized ideological tool of those who seek maximum foregrounding of group division.

Little Audrey doesn't know it, but she is playing with matches. A good guess is that the awards committee at the New York Public Library fully understood this, and they nodded approvingly.

WHITE PRIVILEGE

The most striking innovation in the world of *diversity* in recent years has been the labeling of mainstream American culture as the domain of "white privilege." Recall Obama's 2008 speech distancing himself from Reverend Jeremiah Wright, in which he rejected the "view that sees white racism as endemic." In little more than a decade and after two terms of an Obama presidency, reverend Wright's view is now widely accepted among diversiphiles as true. This has been accompanied by efforts to dismantle English-language terms that enunciate the ordinary state of affairs. Sexuality as experienced by most men and women takes the form of attraction to the opposite sex. The tendency of a society to prefer such reproductive-friendly couplings has been vandalized with the word "heteronormativity." The idea is to suggest we are oppressed when the culture treats opposite-sex attractions as right and proper.

But "white privilege" is the more encompassing term of opprobrium. It is meant to suggest that merely by being categorized as white, individuals enjoy freedoms that are denied to non-whites. Whites move more fluidly through most situations, from the workplace to the supermarket. White interactions with police or state authorities are less fraught with tension. In educational settings, whites are assumed to be intelligent until they demonstrate otherwise. Whiteness confers a "benefit of the doubt" that a member of a minority group seldom enjoys. This unearned privilege seems to the white person natural. It is just the way things are, and he therefore is puzzled when others express resentment of it. His attitude is, "I didn't ask for any privilege. The same rules apply to all. Why are you complaining?"

Once the accusation of white privilege is launched – and it is an accusation – it is difficult to dislodge. The purpose is to shame the white portion of society in an effort to make whites more willing to accept the forms of social reorganization called for by *diversity*. White privilege is above all *unfair*, and a simple demand for justice requires that it be abolished. To abolish it, white people must renounce their privilege.

But can they?

The catch-22 of white privilege is that, once a white person is humbled into accepting how unfair his privilege is, all he can really do is commit to a life of abject apology to his moral betters. This posture of repentance does in fact appeal to some people, though the psychology of it is not as straightforward as just a readiness to defer to non-whites as opportunity arises. That's part of it, but another and perhaps larger part involves the status maneuvers among other whites. The "woke" white person who puts aside white privilege in front of other whites has a claim of superior moral standing.

Declaiming against white privilege has become, for some whites, a status marker. Doing so puts one well outside the "basket of deplorables" and serves as a membership card in the world of enlightened diversiphiles. It has, for example, been taken up by a number of white presidential candidates as a way of appealing to voters.

The notion of "white privilege," like many such ideological follies, is most at home on college campuses, some of which now offer courses on the topic, sometimes based on a "Whiteness Studies" program. Does "white privilege" actually exist? What exists is what is left of a society that has the codes of etiquette and the ordinary manners of an enduring social order. That this order can be traced to the European origins of the United States means that it was formed to a large degree by people who were white. Any social order imposes a degree of conformity on its participants. If someone persistently declines to accept the rules, he will "sink." And over the centuries many descendants of the white European immigrants who created mainstream American society did indeed sink out of sight. They sunk into the urban underclass; they lost themselves in gold rushes; they went whaling and disappeared as beachcombers on Pacific islands; they became foot soldiers in wars on the frontiers, or cowboys destined to short trail drives. "White privilege" was no privilege for most Americans, except that it was an exemption from the chattel slavery of the South. And even that was a thin line. Most Americans, white as well as black, Asian, Native American, and so on, were not especially prosperous or privileged during our agrarian past or in the age of industrialization. The wealthy were privileged, but the privileges of an Andrew Carnegie or Cornelius Vanderbilt were not based on white privilege. They were based on tremendous talent, cunning, and energy.

RACISM

The *diversity* doctrine began as a work-around by the Supreme Court to permit colleges and universities to extend racial preferences to students who were otherwise not qualified for admission to highly competitive academic programs. *Diversity* soon developed a more elastic goal, one which mandated changes in the curriculum, and then became a rallying cry for the transformation of all of American society. But the fundamental if somewhat-buried idea was always to combat racism.

Racism, however, is an elusive target. Simple definitions along the lines of "awarding social goods on the basis of race" or "categorizing people on the basis of race and treating them differently" are stoutly rejected by diversiphiles. Their preference is to define racism as a form of oppression in which a more powerful group disadvantages a less powerful group. By that standard, no one in the oppressed group can be "racist." Lacking the power to oppress, they can only be the victims of racism. By that standard, the dark-skinned man who was walking down Madison Avenue this morning in front of me accosting passersby with, "You're a white n___! You're a Chinese n___! You're a Latin n____!" may have been crazy, but he was no racist.

A new literature that indulges in much the same rant as the gentleman I just quoted, though in slightly more eloquent and academic language, has begun to pour forth from respectable presses. Ta-Nehisi Coates's 2015 book, *Between the World and Me,* inaugurated this new genre of racial screed. It quickly became one of the most widely assigned common readings in American higher education. Reading it, one might think it would be hard to outdo Coates for sheer racial resentment, but he has inspired others to try. The most recent is Ibran X. Kendi at American University. His book, *Stamped from the Beginning,* won the National Book Award in 2016, and his recent book, *How to be an Antiracist,* is a best-seller. *Stamped from the Beginning* offers a version of *The New York Times*'s "1619 Project." America was racist from the word go. Kendi's new book offers his theory of "metastatic racism," which is that racism pervades American society like a cancer. There is no such thing as "not racist." Either you are actively fighting racism or you are yourself racist.[45]

WHITE SUPREMACY

Not that figures such as Kendi see much distinction between "white privilege" and "white supremacy" – both are forms of the "racism" they believe pervades our society. "White supremacy," however, is the stronger charge. It is the claim that large numbers of Americans are committed to a movement aimed at suppressing the rights of non-whites and elevating the political, economic, and cultural dominance of whites. "White supremacy" is a fantasy on the part of diversiphiles who are in need of a sinister ideological foe. Actual self-declared white supremacists exist, but they are fantasists who dedicate themselves to a dream world that ironically resembles that of the diversiphiles. In that world, racial groups differ sharply in their abilities, aspirations, and culture, and thrive best when they wall themselves off from one another.

Further, it is hard to count the number of these self-declared white supremacists. A few thousand? Ten thousand? The combined memberships of the Ku Klux Klan, Identity Evropa, and other such groups is tiny. In the 1960s, the Ku Klux Klan numbered about forty thousand members – even then a marginal group – but the Klan has unraveled since. One observer puts the total of "hardcore" activists in the white supremacist movement at about twenty-five thousand.[46] The Southern Poverty Law Center specializes in exaggerating the number of adherents to the ideology, and to that end lists many organizations as "white nationalist hate groups" that are merely supporters of traditional American values or conservative politics.[47] The accusation also serves others as a weapon against implausible targets. The conservative-turned-leftist journalist Max Boot, for example, attacked *National Review* as a voice of white supremacism.[48] At the other end of the scale is the Fox News commentator Tucker Carlson, who holds that white supremacy is a hoax and claims that "The combined membership of every white supremacist organization in this country would be able to fit inside a college football stadium."[49]

The adherents to the ideology, in any case, are a vanishingly small portion of the American population. That they nonetheless command such a large place in our political discourse reflects the unquenchable need of the *diversity* movement for an enemy to overcome. The supposed existence of a substantial white supremacy movement would give weight and credibility to the broader idea that America is through-and-through-racist. Disagreeing with that conclusion is just a further exercise in "white privilege." Yet many white Americans do disagree. A recent Pew poll found that among white Americans, 56 percent believe that being white helps a little or a lot in "getting ahead in America." Fourteen percent even said being white hurts. Among self-identified Republicans and those who "lean Republican," 59 percent believe that "the legacy of slavery" has little effect on "the position of black people in American society today."⁵⁰

Those who are eager to conjure a view of America as racist, as submerged in unacknowledged white privilege, and indifferent to the hateful schemes of white supremacists can turn these numbers to their own account. Americans are plainly divided about the meaning of our history and the dynamics of our current society. Some see a story of unending racial oppression. Others see the rise of "imaginary oppression" as an identity-forming and identity-reinforcing ideology.

The *diversity* doctrine indeed thrives in the soil of imaginary oppression. Real oppression isn't hard to find in American history or the contemporary world, and the *diversity* doctrine derives some of its emotional power from those real injustices. But the balance of the real to the imaginary, I fear, is that of a grain of sand to a beach. And it is a beach on which crawl a whole menagerie of imaginary monsters.

MONSTERS

The monsters are not hard to spot. Almost every day comes news of a new one.

On August 13, *The New York Times* reported that it had demoted one of its own: a deputy Washington editor named

Jonathan Weisman. He was reassigned to lesser duties because of "serious lapses in judgment."[51] His infraction was in the way he criticized the characterization of Congresswomen Rashida Tlaib (D-Michigan) and Ilhan Omar (D-Minnesota). A progressive Democratic faction in Ohio was planning to run a primary challenge against an incumbent Democrat who is a black woman. Weisman, a staunch liberal, thought that was a bad idea but stumbled by saying that to succeed, candidates in the Midwest need to represent their rural districts. Someone pointed out that Tlaib and Ilhan had been elected in Midwest districts, to which he scornfully replied, "Saying @RashidaTlaib (D-Detroit) and @IlhanMN (D-Minneapolis) are from the Midwest is like saying @RepLloydDoggett (D-Austin) is from Texas or @repjohnlewis (D-Atlanta) is from the Deep South."

The translation is that Weisman was drawing a distinction between the rural Midwest and urban pockets of progressive activism, but his Tweet could be read – if one is determined to find a sinister meaning – as "claiming only rural white people can be 'real' Deep Southerners or Midwesterners."[52]

Weisman was promptly called out as a monster and demoted, though a substantial number of readers believe this punishment was too light. In their view, he should have been fired.

This was a story entirely within the world of *diversity*. Weisman, a diversiphile who has a long record of identity-politics pronouncements and a whole book, ((((*Semitism*))): *Being Jewish in America in the Age of Trump*, devoted to Trump-bashing in the name of opposition to (quoting a review) "the alt-right's embrace of conspiracy theorists," here falls victim to his own enraged cohort.[53] You can be on the side of ever-more divisive identity groups without always being on the prevailing side. The internal battles are sharp, and the cost of losing is steep.

It is well to keep in mind that *diversity*, though it basks in the glow of its supposed tolerance and indulgence of disparate views, is really another soft totalitarianism. And a not-so-soft totalitarianism when it has picked out its scapegoats and its perennial enemies.

Getting named as an enemy is plainly worse.

A professor of engineering at Johns Hopkins University was recently fired for what amounts to a diversity infraction. A group of student protesters had chained the doors of a campus building and occupied it for more than a month. On May 8, 2019, Professor Daniel Povey had had enough and used bolt cutters to break his way through the chains. The protesters apprehended him and forcibly carried him out of the building. They were protesting Hopkins's immigration policies and were concerned that the university was cooperating with law enforcement. For proponents of abolishing boundaries, the protesters had strong ideas about their right to police the one they themselves had created. Because Professor Povey is white and "many of the protesters were black or transgender," Povey was branded a "racist." The university decided he was violent and had "endangered the community." Povey wrote that the students faced little chance of punishment because "Johns Hopkins feared being accused of racism."[54]

Weisman and Povey were not obvious candidates for monsterization. True, both are white males and might be conceived as agents of white privilege ensconced in elite institutions, *The New York Times* and Johns Hopkins Uni-

versity. But they were not tiki-torch bearing white national-
ists or recognized voices of the cis-gendered patriarchy.
They were simply men who for a moment diverged from the
approved narrative on group rights. They were monsters.

The Conversation

A few weeks ago I discussed with some friends the successful lawsuit that Gibson's Bakery brought against Oberlin
College. The college abetted and encouraged students to
label the bakery "racist," after an incident in which a black
student was arrested for shoplifting. The accusation proved
to be baseless. Other students had been arrested for shoplifting, and few of them were black. There was no record
ever of the bakery being accused of racism, and its black
employees testified to the integrity of their employer. The
shoplifter and his confederates pleaded guilty. Gibson's Bakery was simply not a racist institution. In response to the
testimony of the black employees, one of my friends, who
happens to be black, said, "But the absence of evidence
doesn't mean the bakery isn't racist. It can be more subtle
than that."

Points for logic. The absence of evidence isn't evidence
of absence. Common sense, however, suggests that a trial at
which tens of millions of dollars are at stake would have sur-
faced *some* evidence. Unless of course white privilege is so
diabolically woven into the fabric of American life that even
the most ardent investigator cannot pin it down. Though if
that is the case, the massive decades-long effort of diversiphiles to extirpate racial inequity from our society must be
deemed futile.

I am not so pessimistic. In the case of Gibson's Bakery, a jury recognized that Oberlin College had conjured the accusations out of thin air. It awarded the owners of the bakery $11 million – a figure that rose to $33 million as a punitive measure. Oberlin is appealing, of course, but a broader verdict has already been entered among the general public – that the racists in this affair are the diversicrats at the college who unleashed a campaign of vilification against innocent people just to stir the pot.[55]

The truth is that American society was well on its way to freeing itself from the vestiges of racism when the *diversity* movement came along and began to breathe new life into the idea that group loyalties should be primary. *Diversity* is a war on individualism. *Diversity* erodes our rights and redefines our responsibilities away from the love of our whole country and towards the love of that fraction of ourselves that glories in a group. Moreover, the groups *diversity* asks us to glory in are wrapped in stories of mistreatment and injustice. *Diversity* declares pride in the heritage of the group, but it is a pride that is saturated in self-pity and grievance.

That's not an unusual thing in human history. Many tribes and many nations see themselves as victims forever entitled to revenge. But that isn't America. We are the nation of fresh starts, not eternal grudges. *Diversity* is our greatest temptation: an invitation to self-destruct in the name of ethnic pride.

It would be wise to decline that invitation. But it was sent with a kiss, and we are finding it increasingly hard to say no. The better move would be to kiss it goodbye.

Notes

1   Heather Caygle, Jake Sherman, and Laura Barrón-López, "DCCC Faces Mass Staff Upheaval after Uproar over Diversity," *Politico*, July 30, 2019, https://www.politico.com/story/2019/07/29/top-dccc-staffer-out-amid-diversity-uproar-1439525.

2   Jake Sherman, Laura Barrón-López, and Heather Caygle, "Black, Latino Dems Torch DCCC for Lack of Diversity," *Politico*, July 24, 2019, https://www.politico.com/story/2019/07/25/dccc-campaign-black-latino-1435611.

3   Tina Sfondeles, "Madigan Taps Trio of Women, including Bustos, to Change 'Culture of Politics,'" *Chicago Sun Times*, February 18, 2018.

4   Williamson M. Evers, "California Wants to Teach Your Kids That Capitalism Is Bad," *The Wall Street Journal*, July 29, 2019.

5   Teresa Watanabe and Sonali Kohli, "First Draft of State Ethnic Studies Curriculum 'Falls Short,' Board Says," *Los Angeles Times*, August 13, 2019.

6   Dana Goldstein, "Classes Aim to Teach 'History We Don't See,' But Whose History?," *The New York Times*, August 15, 2019.

7   Larry Purdy, *Getting Under the Skin of "Diversity": Searching for the Color-Blind Idea* (Minneapolis: Robert Lawrence Press, 2008); William G. Bowen and Derek Bok, *The Shape of the River: Long-Term Consequences of Considering Race in College and University Admissions* (Princeton: Princeton University Press, 1998).

8   Dion J. Pierre and Peter W. Wood, *Neo-Segregation at Yale* (New York: National Association of Scholars, 2019); Dion J. Pierre and Peter W. Wood, *Neo-Segregation at Wesleyan* (New York: National Association of Scholars, 2019).

9   Thomas J. Espenshade and Alexandria Walton Radford, *No Longer Separate, Not Yet Equal: Race and Class in Elite College Admission and Campus Life* (Princeton: Princeton University Press, 2009), 222–25.

10   Douglas S. Massey, Camille Z. Charles, Garvey F. Lundy, and Mary J. Fischer, *The Source of the River: The Social Origins of Freshmen at America's Selective Colleges and Universities* (Princeton: Princeton University Press, 2003); Camille Z. Charles, Mary J. Fischer, Margarita A. Mooney, and Douglas S. Massey, *Taming the River: Negotiating the Academic, Financial, and Social Currents in Selective Colleges and Universities* (Princeton: Princeton University Press, 2009).

11   Russell K. Nieli, *Wounds That Will Not Heal: Affirmative Action and Our*

Continuing Racial Divide (New York: Encounter Books, 2012), 133, 275, 295.

12   Nieli, *Wounds*, 333.

13   Sander and Stuart Taylor, Jr, *Mismatch: How Affirmative Action Hurts Students It's Intended to Help, and Why Universities Won't Admit It* (New York: Basic Books, 2012), 222–30.

14   Tim Groseclose, *Cheating: An Insider's Report on the Use of Race in Admissions at UCLA* (Indianapolis: Dog Ear Publishing, 2014), 7–13.

15   "The 1619 Project," special issue of *The New York Times Magazine*, August 18, 2019.

16   Gene Dattel, *Reckoning with Race: America's Failure* (New York: Encounter Books, 2017), 267.

17   Dattel, *Reckoning*, 242, 249–50.

18   Heather Mac Donald, *The Diversity Delusion: How Race and Gender Pandering Corrupt the University and Undermine Our Culture* (New York: St. Martin's Press, 2018), 6.

19   Mac Donald, *Diversity Delusion*, 22, 25.

20   John Noble Wilford, "Multiculturalism: Nothing New," *The New York Times*, October 6, 2014.

21   Corinne A. Moss-Racusin, Jojanneke van der Toorn, John F. Dovidio, Victoria L. Brescoll, Mark J. Graham, and Jo Handelsman, "Scientific Diversity Interventions," *Science* 373 (February 7, 2014), 615–16.

22   Gretchen Morgenson, "Not Walking the Walk on Board Diversity," *The New York Times*, May 31, 2014.

23   Nicholas Kristof, "The Diversity of Islam," *The New York Times*, October 8, 2014; Rachel Feintzeig, "Study Finds Diversity Toll," *The Wall Street Journal*, July 23, 2014; Jamal Watson, "HBCUs Challenged to Address LGBT, Diversity Issues," *DiverseEducation*, June 19, 2014; Nikita Stewart, "Stringer Faults New York City on Diversity of Its Vendors," *The New York Times*, October 1, 2014.

24   Clyde Wayne Crews, Jr, "Obama's Legacy: 2016 Ends With a Record-Shattering Regulatory Rulebook," Forbes, December 30, 2016, https://www.forbes.com/sites/waynecrews/2016/12/30/obamas-legacy-2016-ends-with-a-record-shattering-regulatory-rulebook/#53e2af031398.

25   Andrew Sargus Klein, "Obama the Figurehead," *Huffington Post*, May 25, 2011, https://www.huffpost.com/entry/obama-the-figurehead_b_141784.

26   Stanley Kurtz, *Radical-in-Chief: Barack Obama and the Untold Story of American Socialism* (New York: Threshold, 2010); David Maraniss,

Barack Obama: The Story (New York: Simon & Schuster, 2013); David Garrow, *Rising Star: The Making of Barack Obama*, (New York: William Morrow, 2017).

27 Garrow, *Rising Star*, 142, 160.

28 Garrow, *Rising Star*, 177, 163, 161.

29 Garrow, *Rising Star*, 156, 161.

30 Stanley Kurtz, "AFFH Has No Basis in the Fair Housing Act," *National Review*, May 17, 2016, https://www.nationalreview.com/corner/affh-has-no-basis-fair-housing-act/.

31 Stanley Kurtz, *Spreading the Wealth: How Obama is Robbing the Suburbs to Pay for the Cities*, (New York: Sentinel, 2012).

32 "Barack Obama's Remarks to the Democratic National Convention," *The New York Times*, July 27, 2004.

33 https://twitter.com/exjon/status/537007913353883649?lang=en.

34 Barack Obama, "Barack Obama's Race Speech at the Constitution Center," Transcript, National Constitution Center, March 18, 2008.

35 Audrey Hall, "The Book That Made Me Feel I Belong," *Slate*, August 14, 2019.

36 Kevin D. Williamson, "Finding Yourself in an Expanding Universe, Reading Literature," *National Review*, August 16, 2019, https://www.nationalreview.com/2019/08/finding-yourself-in-an-expanding-universe-reading-literature/.

37 Joy Pullmann, "Scholastic's New School Catalog Hawks Books To Saturate Kids With Identity Politics," *The Federalist*, August 21, 2019, https://thefederalist.com/2019/08/21/scholastics-new-school-catalog-hawks-books-to-indoctrinate-kids-with-identity-politics/.

38 Alexander Bolton, "Cherokee Nation: Warren's use of DNA test 'inappropriate,' 'wrong,'" *The Hill*, October 15, 2018.

39 Maria L. La Ganga and Matt Pearce, "Rachel Dolezal's Story, A Study of Race and Identity, Gets 'Crazier and Crazier,'" *Los Angeles Times*, June 15, 2015.

40 Eyder Peralta, "Missouri Football Players Strike To Demand Ouster Of University President," *NPR*, November 8, 2015, https://www.npr.org/sections/thetwo-way/2015/11/08/455216375/missouri-football-players-strike-to-demand-ouster-of-university-president.

41 Katherine Mangan, "Silence Breakers: Concerned Student 1950," *The Chronicle of Higher Education*, December 13, 1915.

42 https://www.thedemands.org/.

43 Wilfred Reilly, *Hate Crime Hoax* (Washington: Regnery Publishing, 2019); Jason Riley, "Hate Crime Hoaxes Are More Common Than You Think," *The Wall Street Journal*, June 25, 2019; Peter Wood, "Fake Crimes, Real Hate on College Campuses," *Townhall*, March 24, 2019, https://townhall.com/columnists/peterwood/2019/03/24/fake-crimes-real-hate-on-college-campuses-n2543594; Amanda Tidwell, "Year in Review: 17 Campus Hate Crimes That Turned Out To Be Hoaxes in 2017," *The College Fix*, December 26, 2017, https://www.thecollegefix.com/year-review-17-campus-hate-crimes-turned-hoaxes-2017/.

44 Dion J. Pierre and Peter Wood, *Neo-Segregation at Yale*, National Association of Scholars, 2019.

45 Jennifer Schuessler, "'Metastatic Racism' May Have a Cure," *The New York Times*, August 7, 2019.

46 Mike Carlie, "Into the Abyss," https://people.missouristate.edu/MichaelCarlie/Storage/white_supremacist_groups.htm.

47 https://www.splcenter.org/fighting-hate/extremist-files/ideology/white-nationalist.

48 John Nolte, "Never Trump Civil War Erupts as Max Boot Declares 'National Review' Alt-Right Site," *Breitbart*, August 15, 2019, https://www.breitbart.com/the-media/2019/08/15/nolte-never-trump-civil-war-erupts-as-max-boot-declares-national-review-alt-right-site/?utm_source=newsletter&utm_medium=email&utm_term=best_of_the_week&utm_campaign=20190817.

49 Quoted from an August 6 broadcast by John Kruzel and Amy Sherman, "Tucker Carlson Says White Supremacy is a Hoax. Here are 5 Reasons Why That's Wrong," *Punditfact*, August 7, 2019, https://www.politifact.com/punditfact/article/2019/aug/07/tucker-carlson-says-white-supremacy-hoax-here-are-/.

50 Juliana Menasce Horowitz, Anna Brown, and Kiana Cox, "Race in America 2019," Pew Research Center, April 9, 2019, https://www.pewsocialtrends.org/2019/04/09/race-in-america-2019/.

51 Marc Tracy, "Times Demotes an Editor Over Tweets About Race and Politics," *The New York Times*, August 13, 2019.

52 Rebecca Fishbein, "New York Times Demotes Bad Tweet Machine," *Jezebel*, August 13, 2019, https://jezebel.com/new-york-times-demotes-bad-tweet-machine-jonathan-weism-1837225569.

53 https://www.amazon.com/Semitism-Being-Jewish-America-Trump/dp/1250169933.

54   Nicholas Bogel-Burroughs, "A Professor Tried to End a Sit-In With Bolt Cutters. Now He's Been Fired," *The New York Times*, August 11, 2019, https://www.nytimes.com/2019/08/11/us/johns-hopkins-povey.html.

55   Peter Wood, "How Oberlin Played the Race Card and Lost," *Minding the Campus*, June 24, 2019, https://www.mindingthecampus.org/2019/06/24/how-oberlin-played-the-race-card-and-lost/; Abraham Socher, "O Oberlin, My Oberlin," *Commentary*, August 2019.